COSTUME AND FASHION SOURCE BOOKS

The 1920s and 1930s

Anne McEvoy

Copyright © 2009 Bailey Publishing Associates Ltd

Produced for Chelsea House by Bailey Publishing Associates Ltd, 11a Woodlands, Hove BN3 6TJ, England

Project Manager: Patience Coster
Text Designer: Jane Hawkins
Picture Research: Shelley Noronha
Artist: Deirdre Clancy Steer

Chelsea House
An imprint of Infobase Publishing
132 West 31st Street
New York, NY 10001

Library of Congress Cataloging-in-Publication Data
McEvoy, Anne.
  The 1920s and 1930s / Anne McEvoy.
    p. cm. -- (Costume and fashion source books)
  Includes index.
  ISBN 978-1-60413-383-7
  1. Clothing and dress--History--20th century--Juvenile literature. 2. Dress accessories--History--20th century--Juvenile literature. 3. Nineteen twenties--Juvenile literature. 4. Nineteen thirties--Juvenile literature. I. Title.

GT596.M385 2009
391.009'04--dc22

                    2009001236

Chelsea House books are available at special discounts when purchased in bulk quantities for businesses, associations, institutions, or sales promotions. Please call our Special Sales Department in New York on (212) 967-8800 or (800) 322-8755. You can find Chelsea House on the World Wide Web at: http://www.chelseahouse.com.

Printed and bound in China

10 9 8 7 6 5 4 3 2 1

The publishers would like to thank the following for permission to reproduce their pictures: Art Archive: 13 *left* (Bibliothèque des Arts Décoratifs Paris/Gianni Dagli Orti), 14 (Culver Pictures), 20, 26 and *title page* (Private Collection/Gianni Dagli Orti), 28, 48 *detail*, 58 (Eileen Tweedy); Bailey Publishing Associates Ltd: *contents page* and 13 *right*, 30 *left*; Corbis: 15 (Bettmann), 22 (Underwood & Underwood), 24 (John Springer Collection), 32 (Bettmann), 35 (Condé Nast Archive), 39 (Michael Childers/Sygma), 48 (Condé Nast Archive), 49 (Bettmann), 54 (CinemaPhoto), 59 (Condé Nast Archive); Kobal Collection: 10 (Universal), 19 (Paramount), 23, 29, 30 *right* (United Artists), 36, 40 *detail*, 42 (MGM), 43, 44, 45 (Clarence Sinclair Bull), 46, 47 (Magnolia/Sweetland/John Clifford), 53 (Warner Bros.); Mary Evans Picture Library: 5 (Illustrated London News), 6, 11 (Illustrated London News), 12, 16, 18 (Illustrated London News), 18 *detail*, 25, 27, 31, 34, 38, 50 (Anthony Lipmann), 52 (Illustrated London News), 57 (John Maclellan); Rex Features: 37, 51; Topfoto: 40; Victoria and Albert Museum: 6 *detail*, 7, 8, 14 *detail*, *title page detail* and 28 *detail*, 36 *detail*, 41, 56 (all V & A Images).

Contents

Introduction

Although the 1920s and 1930s are often lumped together as the period "between the wars," the two decades were quite different in character and styles of dress varied greatly.

The 1920s were the Jazz Age, a period of escapism after the horrors of World War I. The younger generation, especially, turned their backs on the formality and dark, buttoned-up clothing of the previous century. On both sides of the Atlantic, life was now fun, one seemingly endless party. With Europe still recovering from the war and repaying debts, the United States took the lead in new technology. Mass manufacturing made consumer goods cheaper and more accessible. New fabrics seemed to be invented every week—rayon, known as "art silk," nylon, and many more.

In 1929, the Wall Street stock market crash brought the age of reckless partying to an abrupt end. The 1930s began with a widespread economic depression and unemployment and ended with the world at war again. It was a sober period, albeit with welcome touches of glamour for some.

This text brings together some of the most popular styles and dominant trends of the 1920s and 1930s and demonstrates how to achieve the look—from free-spirited flapper to Clark Gable look-alike. Some period pieces can still be found in thrift shops and secondhand sales. Others can be tracked down via the Internet, where auction sites often have vintage pieces selling for low prices. Other items you can make quite simply. Since the 1970s, there have been several revivals of elements of 1920s and 1930s fashions, and these more modern pieces make acceptable substitutes.

Below: This classic outfit from 1929, in black and gold and featuring a bandeau headdress, captures the moment at which the madness of the 1920s began to settle down into the elegance of the 1930s.

ART DECO

The Exhibition of Modern Decorative and Industrial Arts, held in Paris in 1925, spawned the term *art deco*, an artistic style that dominated the late 1920s and the 1930s. Based on geometric shapes and strong colors and inspired by African and other ethnic arts as well as up-to-the-minute technological developments in speed and travel, it influenced everything from architecture and interior design to fashion. Typical shapes are angular stepped blocks, sunbursts, diagonals, and chevrons, but sweeping, streamlined curves are also much in evidence.

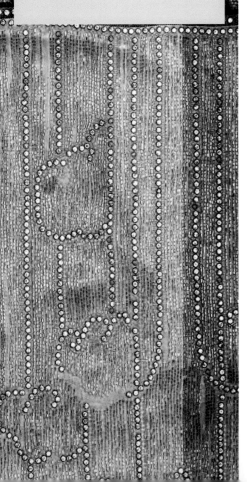

THE ALGONQUIN ROUND TABLE

This was a celebrated group of writers and critics who met every day for lunch at the Algonquin Hotel in New York City to discuss everything from fashion to politics and theater. Members included humorist Robert Benchley; Harold Ross, editor of *The New Yorker*; novelist Edna Ferber; playwrights George S. Kaufman and Alexander Woollcott; and poet and critic Dorothy Parker. They referred to themselves as "the Vicious Circle" because of their barbed jokes and witty gossip.

CHAPTER 1

New Clothes for a New Age

Above: A flapper in a shockingly short dress grabs a ride on the backseat of her beau's bike, indulging the Jazz Age's taste for speed, danger, and fun.

AN ERA OF OPTIMISM

The new decade wasn't called "the Roaring Twenties" for nothing. It was characterized by a relaxation of moral attitudes. The desire to shock, especially among young women, took the form of ultra-short clothing, bare legs, short hair, and obvious makeup. There was optimism, a sense of the world on the move, with air travel, ocean liners, sports cars, and the new, affordable Model-T Ford automobile opening up travel to more people than ever before. Even the dresses moved, with fringes and beads that flapped as their wearers walked or danced. It was in vogue to be "modern." This was also the machine age, a time of obsession with speed and pared-down efficiency. Fashion reflected this by abandoning fussiness and unnecessary detail.

Clothes reflected the new mood of liberation in looser, lighter garments and with a simpler shape. Most dresses were tube-shaped and cut on the straight grain of the fabric, so they hung loosely and didn't cling or follow the contours of the body. The typical 1920s silhouette was straight, boyish, flat-chested, and drop-waisted. It's a great look but hard to live up to for anyone over the age of 25 and weighing more than 110 pounds, so costuming can be tricky.

WHAT WENT UNDERNEATH

Underwear was as sheer as possible. Pantaloons were replaced by loose-fitting cami-knickers or "cami-bockers," a one-piece combination of "directoire" (knee-length) knickers and a chemise. Old-fashioned corsets, which had nipped in the waist and emphasized the hips, were abandoned in favor of a softer version that smoothed the hipline away. The ideal boyish figure needed no real support, and brassieres were little more than lace or cotton "bust bodices" that prevented wobbling, especially when dancing energetically. However, for those with a fuller figure, the fearsome-sounding Symington Side Lacer could help achieve a flatter chest. Today's range of minimizer brassieres will achieve a similar effect with less discomfort, but in 1920, these were way in the future.

HIGH SOCIETY

Despite the revolution breaking around them, smart society, and the older generation in general, still dressed in accordance with the social calendar. They had new outfits for annual events such as the Saratoga or Ascot races and the Henley Regatta in the United Kingdom. Older and more conventional women still changed their outfits several times a day. They had a morning walking dress, an afternoon tea dress, and evening wear for dinner or the theater. And they did mean, literally, a dress: few women wore separates yet, and pants were frowned upon.

THE FLAPPER

The first image that comes to mind when you think of the 1920s has to be the "flapper" girls. The term didn't just refer to their fashionable clothes; it described their unconventional attitudes and behavior. Flappers drank and smoked cigarettes in public, wore

Below: The neat ankle strap on these snakeskin shoes made sure they stayed on during the most hectic dancing.

Below: This fabulous dress combines several typical features of the 1920s—glass beading, a Chinese dragon motif, and a scalloped hem.

makeup, drove automobiles, and listened to jazz. The typical flapper look consisted of a sleeveless, loose-cut dress with a drop waist, reaching to mid-calf. Necklines could be V- or U-shaped or cut straight across the shoulders. Dresses were made from light, floaty fabrics such as chiffon, silk, or the new rayon and often had silk fringes that swung around as the wearer danced. Some were embroidered all over with tiny bugle beads and sequins that caught the light during dancing. Other dresses had just a panel of beaded fabric down the front. They were worn with long strings of pearls and sheer stockings held up with garters that could clearly be seen as the dress flew over the knee in an energetic dance such as the Black Bottom. No wonder people were shocked!

Although there was a silent movie called *The Flapper* as early as 1920, the real flapper era was between about 1925 and 1928. The hit TV series of the 1950s, *The Roaring Twenties*, featured Dorothy Provine as heart-of-gold nightclub entertainer Pinkie Pinkham, whose weekly new outfits were the highlight of the show.

The flapper look is easy to achieve because the shape itself is so simple—little more than two rectangles sewn at the shoulder. It does depend, however, on the fabric. Some 1920s fabrics had abstract patterns, but many were plain, enlivened with the addition of lace, fringes, beads, and sequins for detail. Go for a lightweight silk, silk georgette net, or chiffon for authenticity, but fine crepe is more durable, especially if you're planning beading or metal-thread embroidery. Panels of ready-made beading and sequins can be bought, ready to appliqué. Remember, though, that beading makes a dress quite heavy. The reason so few of these dresses have survived is that the chiffon and net were too flimsy to support the decoration, so they often tore.

HEMLINES

Not all 1920s dresses were short. Hemlines went up and down throughout the decade, so if you're costuming a specific event, check the date carefully. Between 1920 and about 1924, calf length was the fashion, even for flappers. In the middle years, scalloped hems and handkerchief points disguised the fact that hemlines were steadily rising.

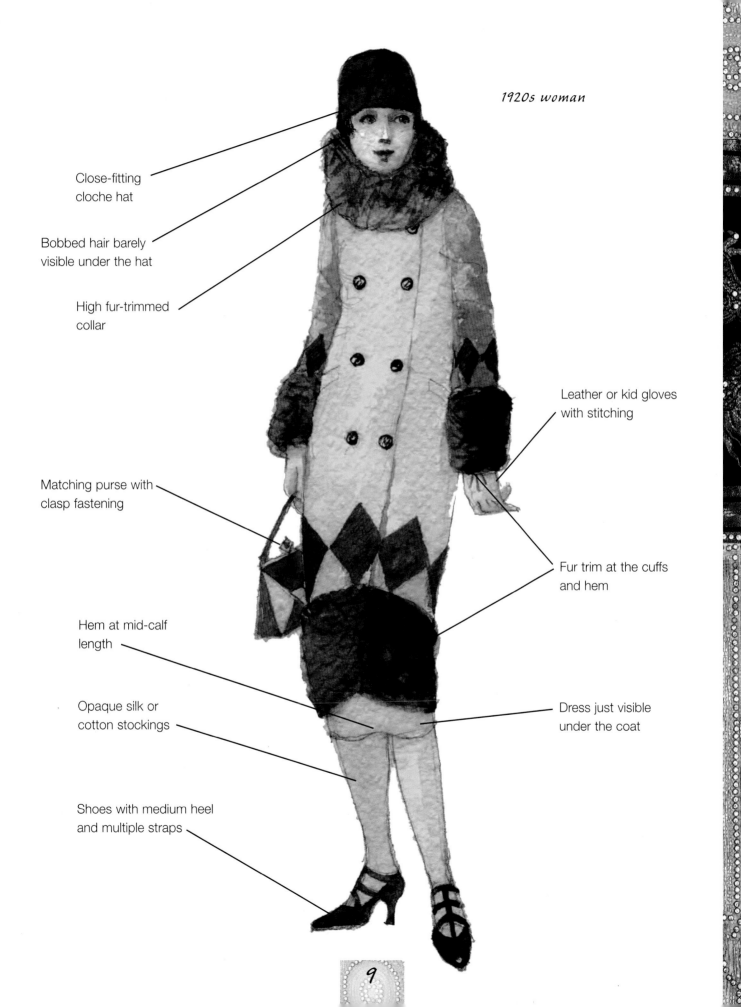

1920s woman

Close-fitting cloche hat

Bobbed hair barely visible under the hat

High fur-trimmed collar

Leather or kid gloves with stitching

Matching purse with clasp fastening

Fur trim at the cuffs and hem

Hem at mid-calf length

Opaque silk or cotton stockings

Dress just visible under the coat

Shoes with medium heel and multiple straps

THE ONE-HOUR DRESS

"A smart, up-to-the-minute dress cut out, completely made, all ready to put on within an hour! You may receive a phone call at one o'clock inviting you to a little impromptu gathering of friends at three, and you can go, if you wish, wearing a dainty new frock made in the time you would ordinarily spend wondering what to wear. Such is the delight you can find in making your own clothes now that it is easily possible to make an attractive, becoming dress in an hour."

Women's Fashion Institute, 1926

Some states tried to fix hems by law at 7 inches (18 cm) from the ground, but, by 1926, skirts were the shortest on record and almost revealed the knees. This was the flapper look at its height. By the end of the decade, however, hems were once again down to well below the knee, with asymmetric designs giving the impression of an even longer look.

Below: In the movie *Thoroughly Modern Millie* (1967), Kansas girl Julie Andrews (right) arrives in the big city to see if those shocking rumors about rising hemlines are true—and finds that they are!

MORE SENSIBLE SOCIETY

In a toned-down form and at a more modest calf length, the drop-waisted look was fashionable everywhere. The low waist was often accentuated with a sash tied around the hips, a belt, or pockets sewn on at that level. A popular variant, worn as a day dress and in the evening, was a straight drop waist with a full skirt gathered on to it. In a soft, floaty fabric, this made a delightful tea dress or a dress for outdoor summer parties. Another version of the same basic style was a perfectly straight dress, given elegant detail by handkerchief-like panels sewn on at the hip so that they hung in folds—this is a very easy way to create a 1920s look. Anyone costuming a show such as *Thoroughly Modern Millie* has a whole range of styles to choose from—the 1920s definitely weren't just about the flapper.

Necklines were generally wide and rounded, but another popular style had a very deep V plunging almost to the dropped waist with a contrasting panel or a pretty camisole filling the gap. Fabrics varied from fine wool and jersey for winter and day wear to silk, chiffon, taffeta, and velvet for evenings. The morning dresses, in jersey or wool, sometimes added a wide, round collar to the neckline. Tiny prints of flowers or geometric shapes, particularly in red, white, and blue, were popular for their clean, fresh appearance. Although the addition of sleeves and collars made these dresses more complex to sew than the flapper outfit, they were still relatively simple—so much so that in 1926, the Women's Fashion Institute offered a design for the "one-hour dress." That's how long it took to make!

COUTURE

Although youth appeared to monopolize the fashion world during the 1920s, there was still a market for couture clothing. High fashion was dictated by Paris via London, and the great fashion houses of Paul Poiret, Lanvin, and

Right: Actor Margaret Bannerman in 1924 wears a longer-length sleeveless dress. Basically the shape is just straight and tubular, with a slash neckline, but it's given extra interest by a silver sash slung low on the hips.

11

Above: This illustration of a fashionable gathering from 1924 shows outfits by top couturiers, including Jean Patou, Paul Poiret, and Georges Doeuillet.

the iconic House of Worth continued to produce Spring and Autumn collections, dressing royalty, European old aristocracy, and American new money alike. Their influence was seen mainly in evening wear, where silk, satin, and velvets predominated. This was one area that offered an alternative to the straight-cut dress. Evening wear was usually cut on the bias to achieve a figure-skimming drape and fit. Clever cutting and seaming were all important and would come into their own in the next decade. Innovative French designer Madeleine Vionnet—"Mme Vionnet"—specialized in these styles, often with the fabric draped from the shoulder into a low back. Evening wear was discreetly elegant, in heavy satins and crepe, with pastel colors such as oyster and pale pinks and blues. Other styles might be draped chiffon with beading or embroidery at the hem or ostrich feather trim. These styles are hard to reproduce, so look out for vintage pieces to buy or rent.

FOREIGN PARTS

There were two exotic influences, particularly in evening wear. The orientalist *art nouveau* influence, which stemmed from the exotic Ballets Russes productions of the pre-war years, was still much in evidence in the shape of Japanese kimonos and oriental patterning. French designers Caillot Soeurs—three sisters of Russian family background—specialized in garments that were hand-embroidered with Chinese birds, lotus flowers, and foliage. Obviously these were specialist fabrics, but if you're

Above: The Egyptian "Pharaoh" look.

Left: The Japanese kimono, with its wide, hanging sleeves.

MAKE IT—A SCARAB BROOCH

Complete your bohemian outfit with a scarab brooch. You need modeling clay and an insect-shaped mold from a child's modeling kit—a ladybug or beetle shape is perfect. Press the clay into the mold and turn out when dry. If you can't find a mold, shape by hand, making simple grooves for the wings and the head. Paint in emerald green and bright peacock blue, then varnish to replicate the iridescent colors of the scarab.

lucky enough to find a printed silk dressing gown in the kimono style or with Chinese designs, this would make an acceptable substitute, especially for a bohemian character.

The other major influence came from Egypt, where the discovery of the tomb of Tutankhamen in 1922 inspired a whole rash of Egyptian-inspired styles. America went crazy over "King Tut": anything in the shape of a scarab beetle, a sunburst, hieroglyphic symbols, or a lotus flower was a must-have. These images found their way onto fabrics and accessories, from powder compacts and lipsticks to brooches and purses.

Gentlemen and Gangsters

MEN OF THE MOMENT

Traditionally, men are slower to change their styles than women. In the 1920s, some older men were still wearing their turn-of-the-century thigh-length swallowtail morning coats, winged collars, and pants without cuffs, especially for formal occasions. Among younger men, though, a more relaxed style was taking over, especially in America. Just like their female counterparts, men wanted to feel less buttoned up. Business suits with short jackets, both single- and double-breasted, replaced the longer frock coats. Made out of wool, serge, or occasionally tweeds, they were more loosely cut, with broader shoulders and wider armholes, and usually worn with a vest of the same fabric. Pants were cuffed and creased front and back. By 1922, the Prince of Wales was ordering all his pants with

Above: The Prince of Wales often went against society's dress code. Here he's dressing down in a shirt and tie with a blazer and white pants.

cuffs, which helped set the style. There was more fabric in them too, with pleats at the waist and fullness in the leg; by mid-decade, they would become extremely wide.

Colors were still fairly conservative, with brown, gray, and dark blue predominating. Patterned silk ties, however, often in the tiny geometric patterns popular in women's fashion, made a splash of color. For evening wear, tuxedos with notched-lapel satin collars, rather than the later shawl collar, were worn with fancy brocade vests. The look was one of understated elegance. Flashier men, especially college types, who overdid it and wore raccoon-fur coats, stylish hats, and patent shoes, were known as "lounge lizards."

BITS AND PIECES

Male accessories were minimal. A pocket watch with a chain looped across the vest was the only accessory many men wore. Jewelry was out—even wedding bands were unusual on men—so make sure your characters remove any of their own. However, for the truly fashion-conscious there were silk handkerchiefs, fringed scarves, and tie pins. And to complete the outdoor outfit of a wool overcoat or Burberry raincoat, a man still needed a hat to raise when he met a lady in the street. There were two choices: the trilby was made of stiff felt, with a narrow brim slightly turned up around the sides and back, while the more raffish fedora was bigger and softer and had a broader brim. It was often worn tipped slightly forward.

Above: The smoldering Rudolph Valentino exploited his Italian good looks, becoming known as "the Latin Lover." Note the jeweled tie pin and unusual pink tie.

BEST-DRESSED MEN

The style leaders, as defined by society magazine *Vanity Fair* in its "Well-Dressed Man" column, were elegant, rather sensitive types. On the international circuit, the playboy Prince of Wales, soon (but briefly) to be Edward VIII, led the field, closely followed by dancer and movie star Fred Astaire and the romantic and brooding Rudolph Valentino.

Below: Any color, as long as it's gray—men's clothing was unadventurous. The boys' suits are essentially the same as their fathers' but with short pants.

THE GANGSTER LOOK

Prohibition lasted from 1920 to 1933 and was intended to curb the immoral behavior generated by the easy availability of alcohol. Instead, it created a ready market in illegal booze and fueled the rise of bootleggers, drinking dens called speakeasies, and a whole generation of rival mobsters vying for control of this lucrative trade. This was especially true in Chicago and New York. Al Capone was just one of the gangsters whose exploits filled the tabloid press, although the movie world wouldn't actually catch up with all this until the 1930s.

A typical gangster look, portrayed in all the classic gangster movies from *Little Caesar* (1930) to *The Roaring Twenties* (1939)—and, charmingly, in miniature form in *Bugsy Malone* (1976)—is a dark suit with a matching vest, a white soft shirt, a showy silk necktie with a diamond pin, and spats. Spats were a kind of shoe protector, usually white, which buttoned over the ankle and looped under the sole. They were probably the last element of a gentlemanly wardrobe to persist into the new age. A silk handkerchief in the breast pocket of the suit is essential for the gangster style, as is a fedora, worn with the brim turned slightly down. Outdoors, you need a dark overcoat, gloves, and a white, fringed silk scarf. You don't actually have to be carrying a violin case, but it's a nice touch. Chicago's most notorious gangster, Al Capone, always made sure he was beautifully turned out for the photographers but preferred them to snap the side of his face that didn't have the scar.

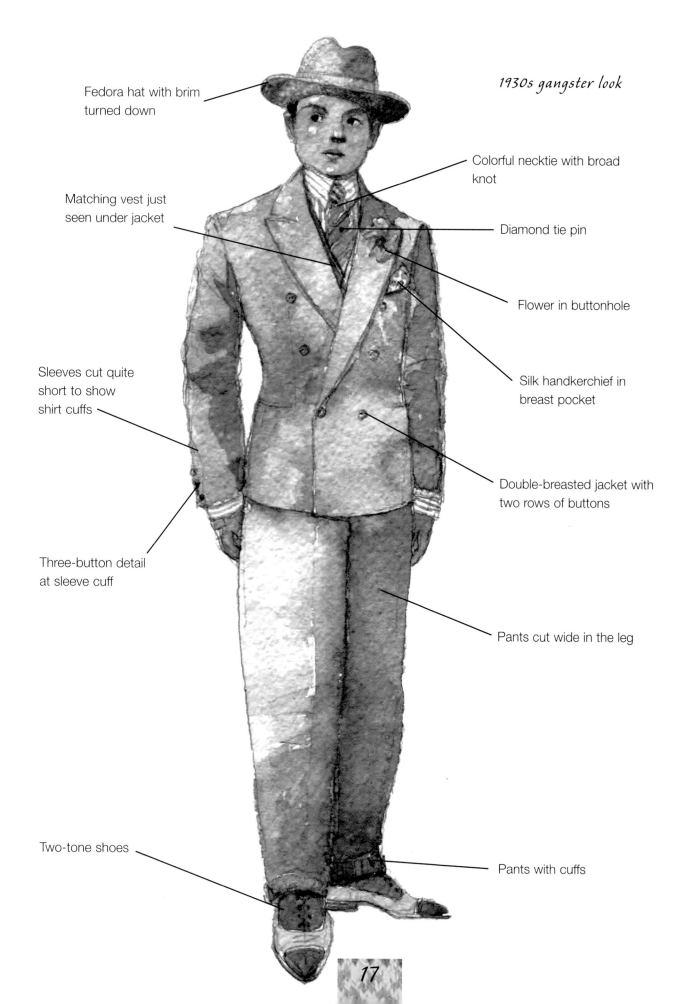

Fedora hat with brim turned down

1930s gangster look

Colorful necktie with broad knot

Matching vest just seen under jacket

Diamond tie pin

Flower in buttonhole

Sleeves cut quite short to show shirt cuffs

Silk handkerchief in breast pocket

Double-breasted jacket with two rows of buttons

Three-button detail at sleeve cuff

Pants cut wide in the leg

Two-tone shoes

Pants with cuffs

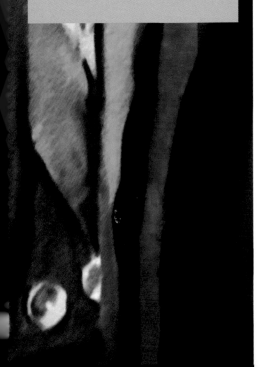

CHAPTER 3

1920s Casual and Day Wear

Women had worked during World War I and developed a sense of independence, which they had no intention of giving up. The new generation of young, free-spirited "office girls" needed everyday, practical clothing. Even middle-class women who didn't work outside the home found they could no longer afford, or find, servants and so were required to do more for themselves. Doing their own housework meant they wanted practical garments in easy-care fabrics that didn't take hours to launder and iron.

Above: These stylish girls, heading for the fashionable resort of Biarritz in southwest France, are wearing a variety of neat cloche-style hats.

Right: The Great Gatsby created an immediate fashion revival of 1920s elegant pale clothes made of linen and floaty chiffon.

QUEEN OF THE SEPARATES

The woman who almost single-handedly revolutionized everyday fashion was "Coco" Chanel. Drawing her inspiration from work clothes and sportswear, she created a range of easy-to-wear jersey suits, cardigans, and pleated skirts that became known as "the new uniform for afternoon and evening." In addition to jersey, she used tweed and other textured fabrics not conventionally thought of as "smart." Flannel blazers, straight linen skirts, sailor tops, and long jersey sweaters combined simplicity with neat elegance, and they suited everyone. A typical Chanel outfit of the 1920s would be a jersey suit, with a long (hip-length) unstructured jacket with patch pockets and a pleated skirt, worn with lace-up flat shoes or low heels. A string of fake pearls and a cloche hat completed the outfit.

MEN AT PLAY

For casual wear, the American college boy look was popular. This consisted of blazers and flannel pants and ascots rather than ties. The ascot is a kind of wide, flat cravat usually worn with a stickpin as part of traditional morning dress and was popular in the 1920s for sportswear and casual dressing.

When the Prince of Wales strode onto the golf course in 1922 wearing a Fair-Isle-patterned knitted sweater with plus-four knickers, he began a craze. Fair Isle, along with the diamond-patterned "Argyle," swept across the Atlantic. Long-sleeved sweaters and sleeveless pullovers, worn with matching socks, became the uniform of stylish men on and off the course.

It was still common for men to have different wardrobes for weekdays in town—suit, double-breasted overcoat, worn with a trilby hat as described earlier—and weekends in the country. In Britain and in much

GET THE GATSBY LOOK

The movie of F. Scott Fitzgerald's classic 1925 novel *The Great Gatsby* brought the 1920s look right back into fashion in 1974. Robert Redford played the mysteriously wealthy playboy Jay Gatsby, and Mia Farrow was Daisy, the elegant love of his life. Both were immaculately turned out, he in linen suits and silk shirts, she in floaty white chiffon. Not surprisingly, it scooped the Oscar for Best Costume Design, despite the fact that because Mia Farrow was pregnant during shooting, her dresses were fuller and more flowing than the true 1920s style.

Fashion magazines were highly influential in disseminating information about the Paris collections. Although *Vogue* remained pre-eminent, the number of magazines increased during the 1920s. These magazines are a mine of information for costumers, both in their features and the advertisements they carry. Other women's magazines featured patterns.

OXFORD BAGS

Oxford bags were the widest, most voluminous men's trousers ever seen! Undergraduates at Oxford University in England began wearing them during the hot summer of 1925, and the fad quickly spread to other colleges on both sides of the Atlantic and to non-university men. They weren't flared but cut wide and loose all the way from the waist. The most extreme were about 24 inches (61 cm) around the hem. Oxford bags were often worn with high-necked sweaters.

Right: For golf, men could choose between long pants, plus fours, or the slightly shorter knickerbockers, worn with long wool socks.

of the United States, this still meant the Norfolk suit, made of sturdy tweed or thick wool. It consisted of a belted jacket with box pleats over the chest and back and matching breeches or knickers. It was worn with wool stockings and brogues; younger men wore it with newsboy caps, older men with a tweed trilby. For many, this was already a conscious anachronism: imitating European aristocracy was something of a fashion. In summer, tweeds gave way to linen suits, in cream or pale shades, with cotton or silk shirts.

Turtleneck jerseys were a relatively new phenomenon in the average man's wardrobe. Having been worn as a naval uniform in submarines and by longshoremen, they were generally thought of as work or sportswear. However, they became fashionable as casual wear when actor and playwright Noel Coward took to wearing one with a blazer: "I was informed by my evening paper that I had started a fashion," he later remarked, feigning surprise.

Short, shingle-cut hair

Short hair worn with part and hair oil

1920s couple

"Sailor" collar on blouse for nautical effect

English-style tweed jacket in country colors

Wool turtleneck sweater

Cardigan-style jacket in navy blue jersey

Leather patches on elbow

Ribbed edging at hem and cuffs

Single-breasted, jacket with three-button fastening

Knee-length jersey skirt

Patch pockets

Silk or cotton stockings

"Oxford bags," cut very wide and straight

Low, "Louis"-heeled shoes with T-bar

Leather brogues

21

Right: In the 1920s, flamboyant French tennis champion Suzanne Lenglen scandalized Wimbledon not just by the length of her skirt but also by revealing bare arms.

SPORTSWEAR

After the privations of the war years, getting fit and healthy was a major priority. This meant lots of sports, swimming, sunbathing, and general outdoor activities. A suntan no longer meant you were a peasant laborer; it boasted that you'd just returned from the French Riviera. Sports had never been more popular, and the same went for the casual leisure clothing that was inspired by it.

Tennis stars Suzanne Lenglen and Helen Wills revolutionized tennis by wearing loose outfits with "short" skirts just below the knee. Lenglen's were designed by Jean Patou, who soon began to incorporate sporty touches into the couture collection. To the great debate on short skirts, Helen Wills added: "Emancipated legs mean better sports." In men's wear, René Lacoste—with his trademark alligator logo—and Bill Tilden

made polo shirts and cable-knit V-neck sweaters extremely popular. Other sports-influenced styles were outfits based on yachting, skiing, riding, and golf. All these offered women the chance to adopt less conventionally feminine clothes. Knitwear became fashionable as outerwear, thanks to these activities, and many women took to knitting their own sweaters and skirts—a welcome change from their wartime knitting of socks for soldiers.

THE BOHEMIAN LOOK

Even before the war, bohemian types had popularized casual clothing—shirts with soft collars, softer and less structured tweed jackets, and so on. In the 1920s, this became more widespread among writers and artists, such as the Greenwich Village set in New York City or the Bloomsbury set in the United Kingdom. For day wear, women took their inspiration from art deco mingled with a kind of peasant chic, wearing strong colors such as purple, red, or peacock blue and plenty of embroidery. They liked to claim they picked up clothing at flea markets, but some of it, at least, was purchased as designer fashion.

Other women went for an androgynous look, which, despite the general disapproval of women in pants, suited the fashionable flat-chested figure very well. Women in tuxedos had an air of gender ambiguity that provided an extra frisson in this endlessly thrill-seeking milieu. Movie star Louise Brooks, one of the period's most beautiful and alluring women, was often photographed wearing a mannish suit and soft shirt or a silk evening pantsuit ensemble that perfectly complemented her short, bobbed, glossy hair.

A bohemian man might be wearing corduroy pants—considered artsy but strange—an open-necked shirt, and sandals, with or without socks. The final touch was that he would not be wearing a hat.

Two ballets summed up the social scene. *Les Biches* (*The Deer*), performed by the Ballet Russe in 1924, shows us a typical society party, with the Hostess in a flapper dress and pearls, a boyishly velvet-suited Girl in Blue, and three

Below: Actor Louise Brooks in one of her trademark silk-and-velvet ensembles. Perhaps she's seeking further art deco design ideas from the theater magazine she's reading.

" Masculine women, feminine men
Which is the rooster, which is the hen?
It's hard to tell 'em apart today!
*   And, say!*
Sister is busy learning to shave,
Brother just loves his permanent
*   wave,*
It's hard to tell 'em apart today!
*   Hey, hey!*
Girls were girls and boys were boys
*   when I was a tot,*
Now we don't know who is who, or
*   even what's what!*
Knickers and trousers, baggy and
*   wide,*
Nobody knows who's walking inside,
Those masculine women and
*   feminine men! "*

Popular song, "Masculine
Women, Feminine Men" (1926)

hearty athletes. Another Ballet Russe hit of the same year, *Le Train Bleu*, immortalized the train that carried the bright young things to the French Riviera. With a story by Jean Cocteau, a curtain painted by Pablo Picasso, and costumes by Coco Chanel, it was as "modern" as it could be. The famous train also starred in a novel by British author Agatha Christie, *The Mystery of the Blue Train* (1928).

GET THE MOVIE LOOK

The movie business was still in its infancy, but already audiences were devoted to their favorite stars, who fell into very obvious categories. These looks are a good party idea and easy to reproduce—just study the publicity photos. The exotic Theda Bara, with her Vaseline-smeared eyelids and smoldering gaze, was "The Vamp"—short for "vampire." Photographs of Bara in skimpy oriental-themed costumes only served to enhance her air of mystery. Clara Bow was the "It" girl (a code word for sex appeal), instantly recognizable by her red cupid's-bow mouth, short

Right: Clara Bow's obviously plucked and re-drawn brows and lashes with heavy mascara concentrated attention on her eyes, giving her a soulful look.

bubbly curls, and daring silk "teddy." Mary Pickford's long, fair curls and wholesome appearance made her "America's sweetheart." She can be paired with her husband, Douglas Fairbanks, who, dashing and athletic, swashbuckled his way through movies such as *The Black Pirate* and *The Mark of Zorro*. A pair of silk evening pajamas will give women the kind of sophistication—and notoriety—actor and singer Gertrude Lawrence achieved in 1926 when she appeared in the Gershwin musical *Oh, Kay!* Silk pajamas, worn as a casual "at home" evening outfit, were considered very "fast" (meaning exciting or shocking).

Silk evening wear for men, on the other hand, was considered elegant and very English. Noel Coward, the English playwright and wit, set the vogue for silk pajamas and, especially, dressing gowns in 1924 when he first came to public attention in America. A paisley silk dressing gown became his signature garment and is a surefire hit for dressing up—add hair gel, a long cigarette holder, or a cocktail glass, and you have an instant character.

Below: This woman's coat, with its panels of folk embroidery, has a bohemian touch, set off by the casual silk scarf. The cloche hat has just the hint of a curvy brim.

WOMEN'S ACCESSORIES

The signature hat for the period was undoubtedly the cloche, a small, close-fitting helmet that covered the newly shorn hair and framed the face. The early styles had a small, upward-curved brim, but by 1928, the brim had disappeared completely. Cloches came in felt, velvet, or varnished sisal straw. For upmarket evening wear, couture milliners turned out orientally inspired turbans and toques to match their dresses.

Although hats were still de rigueur among the older generation of women, many younger women went instead for headbands, scarves, bandeaux, and even fancy combs and ostrich feathers, especially for evening wear. These are easy to make and are the best way of adding authenticity to a costume. A strip of furnishing braid makes a great headband.

Stockings for general wear were made of cotton lisle and were much sturdier than the flesh-colored ones worn for evenings. Today's opaque stockings in various colors are fine: cheating with pantyhose is acceptable as long as you're not wearing a short dress.

Right: Most of the neat clutch-purses, as carried by these two travelers, couldn't hold more than a handkerchief, a lipstick, and a rail ticket. That didn't matter, though, since a porter (or a husband) always carried the cases.

Shoes were generally pointed-toe, low-heeled—known as "Louis" heels—and usually had a T-bar. Modern dance shoes with a low heel are good for this look. Slightly higher heels are acceptable as long as they're stocky: definitely no stilettos. Purses came in various shapes but were generally quite small. The most typical is a beaded or embroidered clutch purse or a rounded one hanging from a chain strap. Vintage purses are still around, but they're expensive and fragile. You can make one using a clasp-and-handle framework available from craft stores and cheap fabric onto which you can appliqué a sequined panel.

Where jewelry was concerned, fake was again the watchword, whether it was ropes of obviously fake pearls swinging from the neck or costume jewelry in the shape of scarab beetles. Following "Tutmania," snake bracelets for the upper arm were very popular. In addition to jewelry, powder compacts, pastel-colored cigarettes in long holders, cigarette cases, and lighters were all must-have accessories that enabled the modern girl to state her independence in public.

HAIR AND MAKEUP

The defining detail of the 1920s was short hair. Depending on how daring you were, there were three styles. The bob, as popularized by

THE PERILS OF THE BOB

"This hair, this wonderful hair of hers, was going—she would never again feel its long voluptuous pull as it hung in a dark-brown glory down her back. For a second she was near breaking down. . . . Twenty minutes later the barber swung her round to face the mirror, and she flinched at the full extent of the damage that had been wrought. Her hair was not curly, and now it lay in lank lifeless blocks on both sides of her suddenly pale face. It was ugly as sin—she had known it would be ugly as sin. Her face's chief charm had been a Madonna-like simplicity. Now that was gone and she was—well, frightfully mediocre—not stagy; only ridiculous, like a Greenwich Villager who had left her spectacles at home."

F. Scott Fitzgerald, *Bernice Bobs Her Hair* (1920)

actress Louise Brooks, was cut straight all around, somewhere between the jaw and the bottom of the ears, and worn with bangs, also cut straight across. A more forgiving style was the shingle, introduced in 1923, which was slightly waved and tapered into a V shape at the nape of the neck. By the end of the decade, the severe Eton crop had arrived, resulting in hair shorter than ever and slicked down. Take a look at performer Josephine Baker for this style. By 1929, the majority of women in America and Europe had short hair. For costuming, as with all hair-related questions, a rented wig is preferable to an impulsive decision.

Men wore their hair in a "short back and sides," parted on the left or right and slicked down with brilliantine, a hairdressing that added shine and kept hair in place. This look was popularized in the early 1920s by screen idols such as Rudolph Valentino. Most men were clean-shaven: beards and mustaches were considered very bohemian.

In pre-war America, "respectable" women were never to be seen wearing obvious makeup. Now it was part of the younger generation's campaign to shock. Plucked eyebrows, rouge, nail polish, and bright red lipstick gave the right "artificial" look that was replacing natural good skin (although a tan was considered glamorous). Kohl around the eyes was essential for the vamp look.

1930s Women's Wear

Above: A wide variety of affordable fashions from a Sears catalog, including the famous "Letty Lynton" style (bottom left).

THE AGE OF THRIFT

The Wall Street stock market crash caused initial panic; contemplating financial ruin, some businessmen took their own lives. The crash was followed by long-term mass unemployment and, for many, grinding poverty. By 1932, 14 million people were out of work in the United States and three million in Britain. In 1934, drought and severe dust storms forced southern farmers off their land. Thousands embarked on the long trek to California in the hope of finding work in the orange groves. This was immortalized in John Steinbeck's novel *The Grapes of Wrath* and in the songs of folk musician Woody Guthrie.

Ordinary people saw their purchasing power diminish overnight. Thrifty makeovers and sew-it-yourself dresses became popular, and a passion for home knitting swept the nation. "Thrift is the spirit of the day. Reckless spending is a thing of the past," declared the Sears catalog for 1930. In general, fashion echoed the more serious mood of the country by becoming sensible and "grown up." Suits, button-down dresses, and generally more severe styles were much in evidence. Hemlines dropped to calf length, and the natural figure was once again visible. A new kind of practical elegance replaced the overheated frivolity of the 1920s—and most women heaved a sigh of relief.

Financial cutbacks in the garment industry meant simpler styles that used less fabric and made do with wool instead of silk. At the same time, technology improved the production of artificial fabrics that were washable and easier to care for. This was important since more women were now going out to work and had little time for hand-washing and ironing delicate fabrics. Even middle-class women were now taking on jobs outside the home, and they needed practical but attractive day wear. As if to compensate for this, evening clothes became more glamorous. Fashion writer Kennedy Fraser has characterized the 1930s woman as "tailored and invulnerable by day, sensual and assertive by night." Something good was to come out of the slump, however, since it forced the big fashion houses to lower their prices and produce more ready-to-wear lines. Fashion started to become more accessible.

A STREAMLINED LOOK

The keynote look of the 1930s is streamlined, a feature that was present in everything—from skyscrapers to trains, Greyhound buses, even radios. Upmarket fashion followed the trend: evening wear was never so elegant, for those who could afford it. This was also the golden age of cinema, and people now took their styles from the movies. Young women scrimped, saved, and sewed to have a dress like Joan Crawford's or Bette Davis's.

Below: Actress Bette Davis in glamorous satin and furs. Davis and her great rival Joan Crawford generally played capable yet vulnerable women who were never less than perfectly turned out.

29

Right: Some Like It Hot (1959) re-created the gangster movie of the 1930s. Despite the similarity of their outfits, somehow the disguised Jack Lemmon and Tony Curtis don't match Marilyn Monroe's style!

Below: The cape-style collar and gauntlet-style cuff were popular details on outdoor wear.

With Prohibition in force until 1933, gangsters were still big in Chicago and New York, but they now ruled Hollywood as well: gangster movies, looking back at the Roaring Twenties, were at the height of popularity throughout the 1930s.

By the end of the decade, the slump was bottoming out, but an even greater horror was unfolding in Europe with the rise of fascism and the Spanish Civil War (1936–39). By 1939, the world was on the brink of another major war, and fashion was once again on the back burner. People had more important concerns.

FORMAL DRESS FOR WOMEN

The 1930s look is slim and streamlined. It's also more adult than the 1920s look. Grown-ups had finally taken fashion back from the flappers. The natural shapes of waist and bust were allowed to reappear, but they were treated more casually: the tightly laced "hourglass" figure was definitely a thing of the past.

Fashion changed surprisingly little throughout the decade: the financial climate meant there was no longer a new "fad" each season. Smart day wear was made of fine wool or jersey and figure-hugging fabrics such as silk or crepe. Skirts were narrow and mid-calf length, flaring slightly to the hem or pleated from the thigh. Jackets had broad shoulders and narrow, belted waists. Clothes came mostly in plain colors, subdued and classic: gray, black, and navy blue for town clothes, with shades of brown and green added for Fall.

RINGING THE CHANGES

Many rich American women were untouched by the Depression and kept up their fashionable dressing, which included changing during the day. A typical range from designer Lucien Lelong included three outfits. First was a morning dress in dark red, with a deep collar tied in a floppy bow and a well-defined belted waist. Afternoon attire consisted of a dress and jacket in crepe marocain, in toning shades of brown and cream, with the loose jacket edged in brown. Last, an evening dress, of "sea-blue lace" with elbow-length puff sleeves, was advertised: "as charming at an

The Material Sets the Hour

Models — LELONG

Left: The three Lucien Lelong outfits for (right to left) morning, afternoon, and evening. A wealthy American woman would think nothing of ordering all three, despite the Depression.

FABULOUS CREPE

Crepe is a woven or knitted fabric with a wrinkled surface that comes in different weights. The finest is silk-based and known as crepe de chine (Chinese crepe); a similar one, popular in the 1930s, was known as "crepe marocain" (Moroccan crepe). Today's stretch crepe fabrics are useful because they hug the figure, but they're not really heavy enough to give the classic 1930s "drape."

informal dinner as in a ballroom" but is hardly what we'd call informal today. This is a good indication that society, at upper- and middle-class levels, still followed convention: costuming for this period demands a degree of formality.

EVENING GLAMOUR

Evening wear was very sophisticated and elegant. A typical gown was floor length and backless, with a halter neck. Another popular style was also backless but had small, flirty sleeves that just covered the shoulders, and a draped cowl neckline. To achieve the requisite figure-hugging quality, these gowns were cut on the bias and featured a lot of diagonal seaming. Bias-cutting means cutting the fabric not on the straight grain but at an angle of 45 degrees. This gives it a natural stretch and allows the fabric to fall easily into folds. It means that not only did these gowns cling seductively to the figure but they could also be slipped on over the head without any need for fastenings. A dress that looked plain and ordinary on the hanger suddenly came to glamorous life when the owner put it on.

French designer Madeleine Vionnet is usually credited with inventing bias cutting, and even if she didn't, she certainly popularized it. French couture still ruled the fashion world. Other famous designers of the period, all expert in the art of draping fabric, were Jean Patou, Molyneux, Lelong, and, particularly, Madame Grès (also known as "Alix").

AMERICAN MASTER

Chicago-born designer Mainbocher produced fabulous bias-cut gowns, first for his exclusive salon in Paris—where he charged his clientele for the privilege of viewing his collections—and later when he returned to the United States and opened a salon in New York. One of his most celebrated clients was Wallis Simpson, who famously said,

Left: Although Ginger Rogers designed many of her own outfits, here she's wearing a Grecian-style evening gown designed by Bernard Newman in heavy pebble satin. The fabric is gathered onto a cord at the neck and falls to the floor in folds.

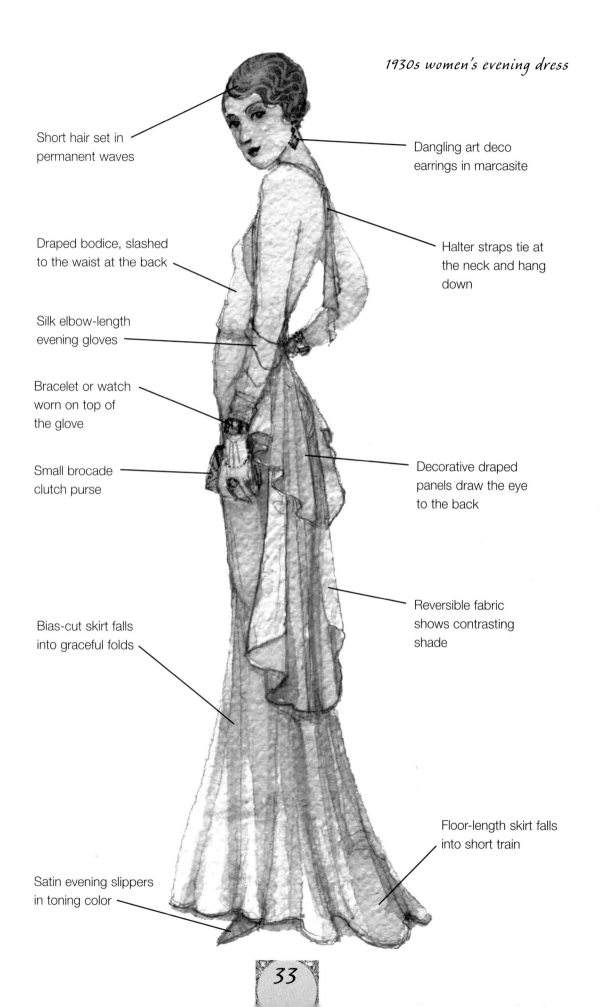

1930s women's evening dress

Short hair set in
permanent waves

Dangling art deco
earrings in marcasite

Draped bodice, slashed
to the waist at the back

Halter straps tie at
the neck and hang
down

Silk elbow-length
evening gloves

Bracelet or watch
worn on top of
the glove

Decorative draped
panels draw the eye
to the back

Small brocade
clutch purse

Bias-cut skirt falls
into graceful folds

Reversible fabric
shows contrasting
shade

Floor-length skirt falls
into short train

Satin evening slippers
in toning color

"You can never be too rich or too thin," and proved it with her own slender frame—perfect for the style of the 1930s. Mainbocher created her outfit for her marriage to Britain's Prince of Wales in 1937 and even invented a shade of grayish blue, which he called "Wallis Blue." He was also the first to introduce the strapless evening gown.

NEW FABRICS

The financial restrictions of the early 1930s inspired designers to investigate unlikely materials. Coco Chanel's 1931 collection, for example, featured outfits ingeniously manufactured from cotton, muslin, and net. Evening wear in artificial fabrics such as rayon increased in popularity. Many of these fabrics are still around today and are of superior quality, so it's easy to experiment if you're planning to make your own gown. Patterns are available online and from most commercial suppliers. Remember, though, that bias cutting is difficult to achieve, even for a skilled seamstress.

COLORS

Pastel shades of peach, pale blue, and pink were very popular and, in complete contrast, metallic lamé. If you're using lamé, it's best to back it with a cotton interfacing: this will prevent too much stretching and will make it easier to handle. Use an interfacing that you can bond by pressing with an iron, but be sure to use a pressing cloth or the metallic fabric will melt.

STUNNING SCHIAPARELLI

Italian Elsa Schiaparelli was a maverick fashion designer greatly influenced by the surrealist art movement. Her breakthrough design was a black sweater with a white bow knitted into it, but she later designed hats that looked like lamb chops, gloves that ended in fingernails, and dresses that appeared to be torn or had strange things sewn onto them—lobsters were a favorite. But she also designed

Left: A 1931 bias-cut gown in peach-colored satin by star designer Mainbocher. The bias cutting is echoed in the diagonal panels of the skirt and the wrap-over bodice.

Above: Seven models wear outfits and accessories by Schiaparelli—suits, dresses, coats, hats, and purses in a variety of fabrics and colors, proving that not all of her designs were eccentric.

ordinary, elegant clothes and was a master of color. Style guru Wallis Simpson owned eighteen of her outfits. Schiaparelli clothes work best on women like herself: petite, dark, and not conventionally attractive. It's a look that demands confidence but will turn heads.

UNDERWEAR

The elegant, smooth look was achieved with long-line girdles made with crossover panels of elastic fiber. These were much more comfortable than boned corsetry and not that different from the models on sale today. Brassieres were back, but now they emphasized the separation of breasts instead of the shelf-like compact bosom of the Edwardian period. This was essential under evening wear. By 1935, American manufacturers had introduced different cup sizes, which made for an even better fit. Today's push-up and strapless brassieres are great under backless dresses.

1930s Men's Wear

RESTRAINED AND RELAXED

In one sense, the 1930s were an unexceptional period in men's clothing. The keynote was uniformity: almost everybody wore the same suit, in a restricted range of colors, and this changed very little throughout the decade. Individual personality was expressed through minor variations in ties, collar studs, and the color of one's shirt. On the other hand, men were more concerned about clothes than they'd ever been, and most men look terrific in suits. Men of the 1930s were well dressed and took care about their appearance. The image they aspired to was that of a strong, relaxed yet confident man who could be depended on to take charge of any situation.

On both sides of the Atlantic, upmarket clothing was much influenced by British style, either in the

Right: Gary Cooper in a three-piece suit and startlingly patterned tie.

Right: Best-dressed "gents" from the movie *Victor Victoria* (1982), set in 1930s Paris.

form of the Prince of Wales, still a leading style icon, or the suave men of the theater, such as Noel Coward, who brought a touch of daring bohemian elegance to an otherwise conventional era.

SUITS

Well-dressed Americans bought their suits from London's Savile Row tailors, as did movie stars such as Fred Astaire, Gary Cooper, and Clark Gable. Cooper was voted "best-dressed man in a suit" for several years running, and costumers can't do much better than imitate him. The new "drape-cut" jacket had a slightly fitted waist, wider armholes, and extra fabric in the shoulders and sleeves, which now tapered to the wrist. This gave a less structured, looser shape that was comfortable to wear but at the same time showed off the natural figure. Pants, worn straight-legged and wide in the 1920s, were now also tapered slightly at the ankle and worn with cuffs.

Suit jackets might be either single- or double-breasted, but they were broad-shouldered and cut quite loose. Double-breasted suits had three pairs of buttons, the top ones just for show, while single-breasted suits had two buttons. Although plain fabrics in gray, navy blue, and brown were in the majority, extroverts might go for a dark brown self-stripe or large, windowpane check in gray. Suits made in fabrics such as these were usually double-breasted.

Businessmen and even men with minor office jobs wore a dark suit with a collar and tie and sometimes a vest. "Dress-down Fridays" were still a long way in the future, and the semi-formal approach extended into weekends, at least in town. Men were rarely seen without a tie.

STYLE TIP

No suit is complete without a folded pocket square in the top pocket. Place your colored square at an angle so that it makes a diamond shape. Fold up one edge to make a triangle and crease the fold. Bring the left and right points in to form an envelope shape. Fold up the bottom edge and turn it over. Place the square in the pocket so the point shows. Choose a color with one of the tones in your shirt or one that picks out a color in the tie, but avoid an exact match. Tie-and-square sets are a fashion disaster.

GREAT TAILORING

Screen heartthrob Cary Grant had a secret that few of his fans were aware of. He was short-waisted but had extremely long legs—at 6 feet 1 inch (1.85 m) tall, he had the legs of a man 6 feet 5 inches (1.96 m). A journalist who gave Grant a lift in his MG sports car noticed that Grant's knees were up against his chin. In order to disguise this, all his clothes, even the casual outfits, had to be custom-tailored. Clearly, the best-dressed man got away with it!

SHIRTS

Plain white or a discreet stripe was the norm, and, although advertising features show a wide variety of colored and striped shirts, checks and other patterns are rare. Collars were generally pointed, although a self-colored shirt, in pink or pale blue with a contrasting white, rounded collar, was also very popular.

Collars seemed to be named for British royalty. The Windsor collar had slightly stiffened points set wide enough apart to accommodate a wide, flat "Windsor" knot in the tie. The Prince of Wales gave his name to a collar slightly narrower than the Windsor and with longer, softer points. In less formal wear, this was worn with a pin that went behind the tie and pulled the edges of the collar together around the knot. Button-down collars on men's shirts were steadily gaining in popularity toward the end of the decade.

COATS

Overcoats either had raglan sleeves, with an overstitched seam down the top of the sleeve from collar to cuff, or inset sleeves with broad padded shoulders. In either case, they had wide lapels, three or four buttons, and either deep, patch pockets or slits. Coats could be straight cut and loose or belted, but fastening the belt with its buckle was for the conventional: for a more individual look, tie the belt in a loose knot. Wear your overcoat with the collar turned up, irrespective of the weather—it just looks good that way.

BLACK OR WHITE, GET IT RIGHT

Business suits were worn for dining at home or at an informal restaurant. Going to the theater or an evening function demanded formal dress. This used to be the bane of a young man's life: it was restricting and unnatural—one of the few leftovers from the turn of the century. Fred Astaire almost single-handedly made evening dress sexy. But there were many variations. "White tie and tails" meant a black tailcoat and dress pants, worn with a white vest, a starched white shirt with a wing collar, and a white bow tie. For less formal occasions, "black tie" meant a black dinner jacket, worn with a white dress shirt and black bow tie. For summer wear, particularly at seaside resorts or in the country, white dinner jackets became

Left: A loose-cut tweed overcoat with raglan sleeves, worn with a fedora, was just as much at home in the country as in town.

popular in the early 1930s, either single- or double-breasted and worn with black pants with a trim of braid down the seam. Another variant was modeled on the short, white mess jacket worn by English officers: waist length and fitted, this jacket was worn with a cummerbund and black bow tie.

NOEL COWARD

English playwright, actor, and wit Noel Coward is famous for his penchant for paisley-patterned silk dressing gowns and silk pajamas. He even caricatured himself in his 1939 play *Present Laughter*, in which he played actor Garry Essendine, addicted to silk dressing gowns. Coward's friend, composer, and movie star Ivor Novello assumed a similar persona in his movies of the 1930s. Although the fashion didn't really take off in everyday America, this is a great character to assume for parties because it's instantly recognizable. You can get away with just wrapping the dressing gown around an ordinary shirt and pants as long as you add a silk cravat and a cigarette in a tortoiseshell holder!

TOP HAT

" I'm puttin' on my top hat,
Tyin' up my white tie,
Brushin' off my tails.

I'm dudein' up my shirt front,
Puttin' in the shirt studs,
Polishin' my nails.

I'm steppin' out, my dear,
To breathe an atmosphere that
*   simply reeks with class,*
And I trust that you'll excuse my
*   dust when I step on the gas.*

For I'll be there,
Puttin' down my top hat,
Mussin' up my white tie,
Dancin' in my tails. "

Irving Berlin, from the movie *Top Hat* (1935)

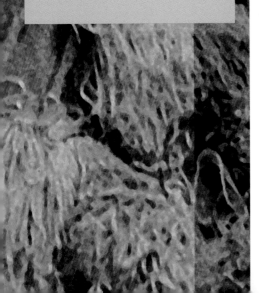

THE SATIN DRESS

" Needle, needle, dip and dart.
Thrusting up and down,
Where's the man could ease a
*   heart*
Like a satin gown.

See the stitches curve and crawl
Round the cunning seams—
Patterns thin and sweet and small
As a lady's dreams.

Wantons go in bright brocades;
Brides in organdie;
Gingham's for the plighted maid;
Satin's for the free!

Wool's to line a miser's chest;
Crepe's to calm the old;
Velvet hides an empty breast;
Satin's for the bold! "

Erwin Blumenfeld, from "The
Satin Dress" (1938)

The Golden Age of Glamour

TYING THE KNOT

Today, many couples choose a 1930s-themed wedding because the outfits are so elegant. Whether for a church or a civil marriage ceremony, wedding gowns tended to be floor length, often extending into a train, and bias-cut to be figure-skimming, like evening gowns. Cream or white satin was overwhelmingly the favorite fabric, sometimes embroidered with flowers or trimmed with net but often left quite plain. Bear in mind, though, that unless you have a very slim figure, plain white satin is a very revealing fabric. A short bolero is an extra touch, perhaps with pearls or a metallic embroidery feature on the shoulder. In the 1930s, most brides would have worn a net veil. Gloves were optional: the only guide is, the shorter the sleeve, the longer the glove. Wedding shoes were metallic silver or gold, with a medium heel—no stilettos.

The wedding dress code for the groom and groomsmen was more complicated. Strict etiquette stated that "no man should ever be seen in a church wearing a tuxedo," but the trend toward relaxation of these rules was creating a need for "semiformal" wear. A 1937 advertisement for

Above: A typical wedding group, with bride and bridesmaids in plain satin.

men's wedding clothes shows a bewildering number of variations. For a formal daytime ceremony, a morning (swallowtail) coat was worn with a vest, striped pants, and a top hat. For an evening ceremony, it was white tie and tails but no hat. For an informal town wedding in daytime, a double-breasted gray or cream suit, white shirt, gray check ordinary tie, and black patent leather shoes would do. If it were an evening ceremony in town, a black tuxedo and bow tie would be worn, but for a country affair, a semi-formal white tux jacket, black pants, and bow tie would do just fine.

BRIDESMAIDS AND GUESTS

Bridesmaids' dresses were often confections of tulle or net in summer and velvet in winter. They were rarely in the same satin as the bride's. The soft neutral tones of beige and lavender, popular in the 1920s, had given way to stronger shades of rose-pink and purple, but they were still quite muted, so avoid bright colors. Guests should observe the same general etiquette: ladies should wear hats and perhaps carry a parasol, and gentlemen's suits should correspond to the time and place. Weddings, of course, are a minefield. If you're planning a real one, you may want advisers or a rental company to guide you. If you're costuming for the stage, consider this a good starting point.

THE SILVER SCREEN

This was the golden age of cinema, and movies are a great source of inspiration for the costumer. Modern movies, such as *Gosford Park* (2001) and *Atonement* (2007), keep revisiting the 1930s simply because the clothes are so elegant,

Right: This elegant bridal gown is in patterned ivory silk shading into an extended train of tea-colored tulle.

while movies made at the time were watched as much for their fashion style as for the story. Many of them were fantasy adventures and historical romances, designed to keep the audience's mind off the Depression—there were monster movies such as *Frankenstein* and *Dracula* (both 1931), screwball comedies such as *Bringing Up Baby* (1938), and zany musical comedies such as *The Gay Divorcee* (1934). Most important, though, was the glamour. Both sexes took fashion cues from their favorite stars, and women flocked to local stores in the hope

Right: Joan Crawford in the famous "Letty Lynton" dress. Although not conventionally beautiful, Crawford used her clothes to great effect and always appeared glamorous.

THAT DRESS

The "Letty Lynton" dress created a sensation in 1932. Macy's in New York reported selling over half a million similar dresses in that store alone. It was a white organdie dress with wide shoulders, extravagantly ruffled sleeves, and a nipped-in waist. It was a dress much imitated by bridesmaids and prom queens and is a good style for either of those today.

of finding a replica of the dress worn in the latest movie drama by Bette Davis or Joan Crawford.

Although costume designers based their work on current couture, very few fashion designers actually worked in movies themselves. Coco Chanel was the exception, designing costumes for several movies, including *Le Quai des Brumes* (*Port of Shadows*) (1938) and *La Règle du Jeu* (*The Rules of the Game*) (1939).

One of the most famous movie costume designers was Adrian, who worked for MGM studios. He worked on over 200 movies, making gowns for Joan Crawford, Greta Garbo, and Jean Harlow in particular. He created the "Letty Lynton" dress for Crawford in the movie of the same name (1932) and the "Eugenie" hat for Garbo in the movie *Camille* (1936).

BLONDE BOMBSHELLS

Mae West, with her voluptuous figure, was Hollywood's most controversial—and popular—star. In *I'm No Angel* (1933), everyone's favorite "bad girl" coined the famous phrase: "When I'm good, I'm very good. But when I'm bad, I'm better." For the Mae West look, you need a figure-hugging, floor-length gown with a very low neckline and the figure to fill it. A fishtail train and lots of feather trim will work well. Because West looked younger than her years (and notoriously lied about her age), her style can be adapted by a wide age group, but it's not for the faint-hearted.

FINE FEATHERS

The "Blonde Bombshell" look of Jean Harlow is less outrageous than that of Mae West. To achieve it, slip into a bias-cut satin gown, preferably with lots of marabou trimming, and a short ash blond wig set

Above: Mae West's hourglass figure was the model for a Schiaparelli perfume bottle.

Be a blonde! Blonde hair became ultra-fashionable, especially the obviously dyed, almost white "platinum blonde" made famous by glamorous Jean Harlow in the 1931 film of the same name. For real authenticity, the hair should be bleached with repeated treatments of peroxide, but fortunately much less damaging products are around today, and wigs are an even better option.

Right: Katharine Hepburn relaxing between takes with her knitting and in her favorite slacks outfit. Her "look" was unconventional then but wouldn't raise an eyebrow today.

in permanent waves. Marabou feathers were very popular in the 1930s. These very fine, fluffy feathers that seemed to float in the air were usually dyed in pastel colors and worn around the neck or cuffs or on a headband. They are available from bridal suppliers and some craft stores and will add instant glamour to a gown.

TAKE YOUR PARTNERS

Dancing was a passion in the 1930s, both in dance halls and on-screen. Dance movies with Fred Astaire and Ginger Rogers were full of glamorous clothes—Fred in white tie and tails, Ginger in an assortment of gowns she designed herself. Fred-and-Ginger is a great look for theme-party couples and easily attainable, but it's wise to take some dance lessons first in case people expect you to live up to the image.

GIRLS IN SLACKS

While many of the screen goddesses played on their femininity, others, such as Marlene Dietrich and Katharine Hepburn, were more adventurous and were often seen in rather masculine outfits—in which, of course, they looked just as good. If frilly isn't your thing, then a well-cut

pantsuit worn with a soft shirt, or slacks and a sweater will give you the look. Hepburn made the most of a rangy, athletic figure and refused to be stereotyped as a "clotheshorse," claiming instead that she dressed for comfort. When an angry studio boss took away her slacks, Hepburn walked around the lot in her underwear until he gave them back.

Top hat and tails, paired with a blonde wig and sultry eye makeup, will identify you more quickly as Marlene Dietrich than the slinky evening gowns she also wore. The German-born Dietrich made her mark in 1930 as Lola Lola, a Berlin cabaret singer, in *The Blue Angel*.

QUEEN OF MYSTERY

Greta Garbo was promoted by the studios as an exotic and serious, even tragic figure. Many of her roles were as foreign beauties in historical dramas—a Russian ballerina in *Grand Hotel* (1932), Queen Christina of Sweden (1933), and the mysterious spy in *Mata Hari* (1931)—so her signature style is harder to pin down. However, a tailored suit with a fur

Left: Greta Garbo specialized in hats and berets of all kinds. Close-fitting models like this, however, can be unforgiving to those who aren't lucky enough to have her perfect bone structure.

wrap and a slouch hat—a larger version of the 1920s cloche—pulled slightly down over one eye and showing a pageboy haircut should do the trick. Oh, and a Swedish accent!

ALL-AMERICAN BOYS

Paris couture may have ruled in the female wardrobe, but a sense of homegrown American style was becoming apparent in men's wear as the new movie heroes made their mark. After the sensitive souls of the 1920s, cinema's leading men were now more athletic and more manly.

Top suave-suited heroes Cary Grant and Gary Cooper made the most of the broad-shouldered cut of classic men's tailoring and were rarely seen in casual dress. To get the Grant-Cooper look, men simply need to be immaculately turned out in a suit and tie, with short hair. They should also be holding a cigarette, even if it isn't lit: in the 1930s, smoking was considered the height of "cool," particularly for men.

Right: Clark Gable managed to make "casual" mean attractive. The world's biggest movie star and "King of Hollywood" throughout the 1930s and 1940s, he used to say, "I'm just a lucky slob from Ohio."

STYLE TIP

In the 1934 movie *It Happened One Night*, Clark Gable took off his shirt for bed and revealed a bare chest. Apparently, sales of undershirts slumped as American men threw away their underwear in imitation of their hero. Whether or not this is true, that movie moment established Gable as the biggest sex symbol of the day and "King of Hollywood." So if you're going as Gable, leave the undershirt or T-shirt at home.

Clark Gable had a rough-hewn, "regular guy" appeal. He was more likely to be seen in casual clothes than Grant or Cooper, although he was equally at home in evening dress. Gable made six movies with Jean Harlow, and their on-screen chemistry caused audiences to swoon. This would be another good idea for a party couple. For the Gable look, you need a neat, pencil-slim mustache and slightly oiled and carefully tousled hair. You can either go in casual mode, which means sleeves rolled up above the elbow, or smart in a suit. The only role to avoid is his most famous one—Rhett Butler in the Civil War epic *Gone With the Wind* (1939)—which means historical costume, not 1930s.

GANGSTER CHIC

Gangster movies such as *Little Caesar* (1930) and *Public Enemy* (1931) were hugely popular, but by 1933, the government felt they had gone too far in portraying brutal violence and bad language. The new Hays Code banned weapons, the killing of police officers on-screen, and any suggestion that criminals got away unpunished. To get around this, movies presented gangsters as victims of society, and they acquired a new respectability.

Below: Director Woody Allen set his 1999 movie *Sweet and Lowdown* in the 1930s, inventing a fictional musician (Sean Penn, center) to investigate the Depression music scene. Although New York had to stand in for the Chicago and San Francisco locations, the costumes are authentically 1930s.

1930s Day Wear, Sportswear, and Children's Wear

CLOTHES FOR EVERY DAY

For women, casual and day wear followed the same general line as formal wear. Skirts were narrow and calf length; jackets had broad shoulders. However, longer, straight cardigan-style jackets, made of soft wool or jersey, were fast gaining in popularity. Tweeds and wool mixes in contrasting weaves were also widely used.

This was the era when separates really came into their own. People who could no longer afford a whole new outfit managed to update their

Below: Neat separates for everyday wear: a cashmere dress and cardigan-style jacket in neutral colors.

existing one with accessories or a new blouse. And of course many people were still wearing their 1920s styles.

MAKING DO

Cash-strapped women became adept at restyling old garments, adding trimmings and sometimes lengthening a skirt by adding a contrasting panel. Because these efforts were all too obvious, this is a good way of indicating a character's changed circumstances or lowered social status in plays about the Depression. People also shopped at secondhand stores in an attempt to keep up appearances, so a character might be wearing something that appears to be out of her usual class—for example, a fur or a hat.

KNITWEAR

Without a doubt, this was the decade of knitwear. Imported European woolens were fashionable but expensive, so home knitting became a craze, followed swiftly by an increase in commercially produced knits for all members of the family. Sweaters, cardigans, cobweb-lacy tops, suits, berets, gloves, beachwear, and even swimwear clicked off the needles. "If you do not have at least one knitted costume in your wardrobe today," warned *Gentlewoman* magazine, "something is wrong." The only problem was the name. British "Guernseys" (pullover style) or "Jerseys" (button front) were just "sweaters" in the United States, which gave rise to concern among some who felt that the name sounded indelicate, as it suggested perspiration. Whatever they called it, more and more American women were knitting their own. Knitwear is a real 1930s style signature. There's no quick way to knit a sweater, but vintage patterns are easily available.

THE TOMBOY LOOK

Free-thinking women took up the style of female flying ace Amelia Earhart, who was often photographed near her airplane wearing a leather jacket, slim pants, and a selection of silk ties. She carried off the tomboy look brilliantly, thanks to her slight frame and short, tousled hair. She's a great character to costume. Along with Katharine Hepburn, Earhart did much to overturn

Right: Amelia Earhart made the most of her petite figure in a leather jacket and jodhpur-style pants, often worn by pilots in the early days of flying.

the long-standing ban on women in pants and make them socially acceptable. Amelia Earhart launched her own fashion collection in 1934, featuring her trademark smart-casual, rather masculine outfits.

DRIVING

Now that more people had cars, driving excursions were popular. The correct outfit for a weekend driver—almost always the man of the family—was a single-breasted jacket and slacks and maybe a hat, unless he was driving an open-top sports car. The woman in the passenger seat wore a neat suit and a hat or, if the weather was chilly, a trench coat or the new three-quarter-length swagger coat (these were the height of fashion by about 1938). Leather and suede jackets were also recommended as driving wear, worn belted and teamed with a tweed skirt.

MEN

Off duty, or in the country, men wore open-necked shirts (sometimes with a cravat), roll-neck sweaters, baggy corduroy or loose, pleated cotton pants, and sports jackets or blazers. Sports jackets usually had two buttons, single pockets with flaps, and broad, semi-notched lapels. Leather jackets were also popular, although they were for the more unconventional males.

Below: Skiers arrived on the slopes wearing pretty much what they'd wear for any other outdoor sport. Safety obviously wasn't an issue in those days.

Right: In the 2007 movie *Atonement*, set in the 1930s, Keira Knightley wears one of the new, daringly figure-hugging bathing costumes.

The introduction of elasticized waistbands made casual pants more comfortable, especially for informal sporting excursions. By now, most pants had a zipper fly rather than buttons, and they were kept in place on the waist by belts rather than suspenders. Generally, pants were worn higher on the waist than they are today.

Even in informal situations, it was still considered slightly uncouth for a man to be hatless. Hats should be worn tipped forward and raised courteously when a lady appears: lessons in old-fashioned etiquette may be in order here.

SPORTSWEAR FOR ALL

During the 1930s, the production of active sportswear boomed, with manufacturers developing new fabrics that made costumes both comfortable and more efficient. Commercial sportswear continued to be promoted by the sports personalities themselves, many of whom went into the movies after retiring from competition. Even people who didn't actually take part in sports wanted to be seen in sporty clothing. As hemlines of day and evening wear dropped, sportswear became steadily more revealing, showing legs and shoulders in ever more daring ways.

ON THE SLOPES

Skiing was taking off in a big way in America, partly as an alternative way of getting that "healthy" outdoors tan. Skiing outfits were sleek and streamlined but nothing like the all-in-one quilted suits of today. Norwegian pants with knitted or elasticized cuffs were worn with sweaters and a short boxy jacket on top. Ski sweaters were either in the Fair Isle pattern or had jaunty motifs of snowflakes or skiing figures knitted in.

BY THE SEA

By the middle of the 1930s, men and women were wearing one-piece bathing suits cut to the top of the leg, and it was even considered respectable for men to swim in mixed company wearing only swimming trunks. The costumes were made of new figure-hugging knitted fabrics such as Lastex.

ICE QUEEN AND MERMAID

When ice-skating champion Sonja Henie retired from competition in 1936, she began making movies featuring balletic skating sequences in which she wore designer outfits with daringly short pleated or flared skirts. Henie was soon the highest-paid screen star of the day and made ice skating popular all over America. By the end of the decade, Esther Williams was doing the same for swimming, in movies that featured synchronized water ballets and a succession of elegant swimsuits.

DOWN TO THE SEA
IN SHIPS:
SUMMER HOLIDAY
FASHIONS.

Above: The nautical look was one of the key fashions of the 1930s, even among ordinary people, who couldn't afford to go on a cruise.

In order to keep their suntans, people needed to spend more time on the beach. Those who didn't want to swim strolled about in chic beach pajamas. Widely flared in the leg and made in heavy crepe de chine, they hung beautifully. A good outfit for a character by the seaside or on a cruise is a pair of sailor pants, flat-fronted and with a buttoned panel, worn with a blue-and-white top or naval jacket. Nautical colors of navy and white, with touches of bright red, are the keynote of seaside wear, along with a jaunty straw hat.

PLAYING BALL

Tennis outfits became shorter and shorter. French star René Lacoste's short-sleeved shirts were already established, and in 1932, Bunny Austin appeared at Forest Hills in shorts, finally banishing the long flannel pants worn up until then. The following year, Alice Marble wore shorts at Wimbledon and caused a sensation. Tennis had come a long way from Helen Wills's "short" knee-length skirts.

In the 1920s, the Prince of Wales had been instrumental in popularizing plus-four pants, so called because they are cut 4 inches (10 cm) below the knee. Already traditionally worn by golfers, they had also been accepted as weekend wear in the country. By the 1930s, this was considered old-fashioned and plus fours were relegated strictly to the golf course. Women played in pleated tweed skirts or culottes.

DANCING

One of the few recreations almost everybody could afford was dancing. It was the major social activity, after going to the movies. People dressed their best to go to the dance hall, although few managed the full Ginger Rogers look. Most women wore a neat skirt and blouse, while their partners settled for a suit with comfortable shoes.

Some of the most bizarre events of the Depression era were the marathon dancing competitions made famous in the movie *They Shoot Horses, Don't They?* (1969). Competing for cash prizes, couples dragged themselves around a ballroom continually for days and even weeks at a

Left: The Aviator (2004) followed the career of reclusive millionaire Howard Hughes from the late 1920s to the mid-1940s. Here we see Leonardo DiCaprio as Hughes and Cate Blanchett as Katharine Hepburn in one of the 1930s scenes. Both are wearing casual everyday outfits.

time, eating and drinking on their feet: the last couple left standing won. The authorities tried to ban these events, but with a modest entrance fee and prizes as much as $5,000, they were popular. It also gave homeless couples a few nights of warmth and shelter.

CHILDREN

Children's wear was not nearly as imaginative as it is today. In an era when children were still supposed to be "seen and not heard," it was quite formal. The keynote for girls was short—well above the knee—and almost certainly a dress rather than a skirt and blouse; no pants, and certainly no jeans. Smocking on the bodice was popular, as was piping around the edges of the collar and yoke. Wool dresses with box pleats were popular for winter, replaced in summer by cotton poplin or striped batiste sundresses in pastel shades of pink or blue with white Peter Pan collars. Most girls wore white ankle socks and laced or T-bar shoes or knee-

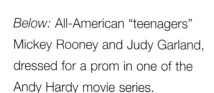

Below: All-American "teenagers" Mickey Rooney and Judy Garland, dressed for a prom in one of the Andy Hardy movie series.

length boots in winter. Coats were also short, with velvet collars and matching covered buttons, and even quite small girls wore hats. Cloche-style felt hats were popular for pre-teens.

Boys' clothes were rather like their fathers'. It wasn't unusual to see a very small boy in a velveteen coat in the 1930s, but most ordinary boys wore suits like their fathers, with long pants.

SCREEN TOTS

However, even children—or more likely their mothers—took their style cues from the movies. Every little girl wanted to look like Shirley Temple or, if a little older, Judy Garland or Deanna Durbin. Boys went for the Mickey Rooney look.

Shirley Temple was the most famous child star of all time, singing and tap dancing her way through a whole series of movies, bolstering the morale of Americans throughout the Depression and prompting President Franklin Roosevelt to say, "As long as our country has Shirley Temple, we will be all right." She was also big business: Temple-themed fashion products were everywhere, ranging from replicas of her dresses, hair ribbons, bracelets, and handkerchiefs to dolls dressed in costumes from her movies. These dolls are collectors' items today and fetch high prices, but the Web site catalogs are a good fashion resource.

The two English royal princesses, Elizabeth and Margaret Rose, were also style setters. In 1932, the "Margaret Rose" dress, trimmed with the princess's favorite rosebuds, swept the western world.

"REAL" LIFE

A good visual source for "ordinary" clothing is the series of Andy Hardy films made during the 1930s. They feature an ordinary American family, with young Mickey Rooney as Andy, the exuberant, wisecracking, all-American teenager (although the term teenager hadn't been invented yet). He's usually dressed in a plaid sports jacket and tie—hardly the uniform of rebellious youth. A good party double act for a teen boy and girl would be Andy Hardy and his long-suffering girlfriend, Polly. Or you could costume the whole family and go as a group.

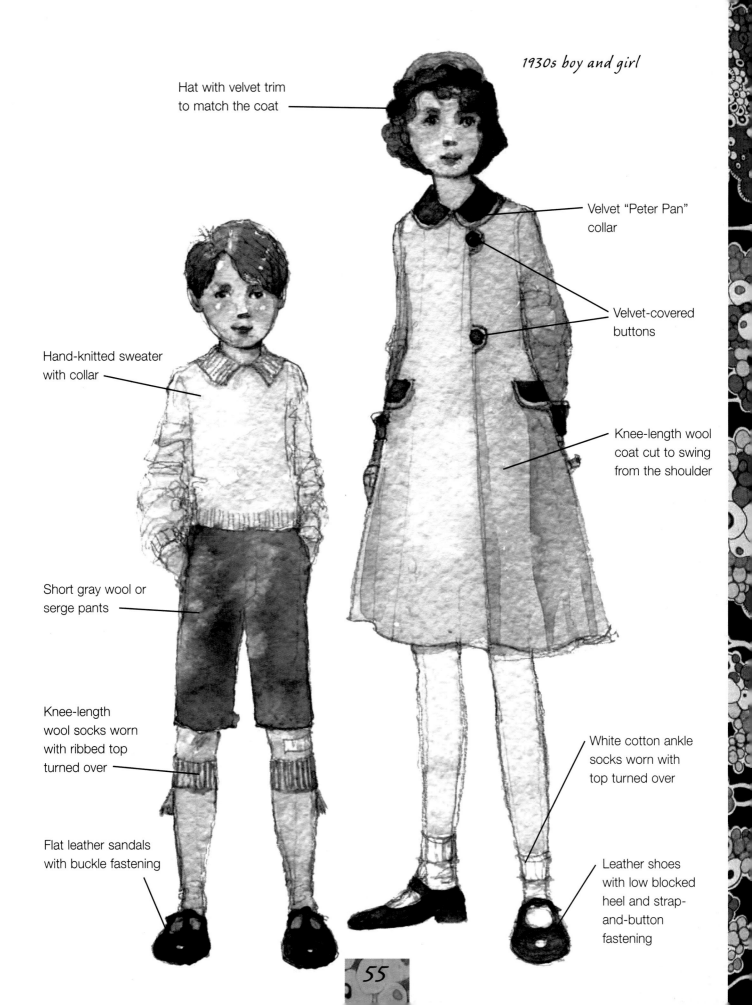

Hat with velvet trim
to match the coat

1930s boy and girl

Velvet "Peter Pan"
collar

Velvet-covered
buttons

Hand-knitted sweater
with collar

Knee-length wool
coat cut to swing
from the shoulder

Short gray wool or
serge pants

Knee-length
wool socks worn
with ribbed top
turned over

White cotton ankle
socks worn with
top turned over

Flat leather sandals
with buckle fastening

Leather shoes
with low blocked
heel and strap-
and-button
fastening

Below: Note the bizarre bird's head nestling among the feathers on this otherwise quite straightforward black straw hat!

MAKING DO WITH DETAILING

In a period when people couldn't afford new outfits, accessories became all important. As in earlier periods, men were slow to take up the challenge of fashion and were less concerned about updating their image. However, they did venture as far as leather gloves, silk scarves, shirt studs, and cuff links.

Hats were major fashion items and came in dozens of styles. On the whole, though, women's hats were small, jaunty, and rather masculine. Informal or daytime hats were usually made of felt and had a band. A Tyrolean style with feathers was very popular. Others, especially those worn in summer, were made of glazed straw. Both styles were sometimes worn with a short net veil over the forehead and eyes. Younger women favored the pull-on beret styles, and the slouch hat made famous by Greta Garbo was popular when worn with a suit or a trench coat. Whatever the style, hats were generally worn at an angle. Deco-style hat pins, with large glass baubles, were a fashionable way of keeping the hat in place. These are much sought after now, and if you can find them, they're great accessories. Ultra-fashionable hats ranged from the pillbox toque to the velvet-trimmed turban and Basque beret. Patterns for vintage hats are available online.

Men's hats fell into two quite similar styles: the trilby and the fedora. Both were soft felt hats with a flexible brim and an indented crown. The trilby was a European hat, named after a character in a play in which the style was first worn, while the fedora was an American style. The fedora had a slightly wider brim than the trilby, but they were both worn tipped slightly forward, with the brim up at the back and down at the front. They came in gray, brown, and black, with a matching band.

SHOES

Women's shoes were much more interesting than they had been in the 1920s. There was a choice of flats, for both day and evening, sandals, wedges, or slingbacks. Heels were higher and more slender to suit the elongated line of the dress, although the stiletto was still a long way in the future. Plain leather pumps with a moderate heel would be perfect for most outfits, while lace-ups and buckle shoes were all worn for every day. Older women might go for a rounded toe with a wide, thick heel. There was also a brief fashion for two-tone "spectator" shoes. By the end of the decade, however, everyday shoes had become a little clumpy and unattractive.

PURSES

Daytime purses came in many styles but were mostly quite small, square, and neat—the streamlined look of the period. Some had a flap and fastened with a catch, while others had a snap fastening on the top edge; zippers were rare. Purses either came with short handles or as a clutch style, with no handles. Shoulder bags were very rare in this period. Purses might be in plain colored leather, tooled leather, or crocodile skin for daytime but were always chosen to match the suit or coat. It was very much "the thing" to have purse, shoes, and gloves all perfectly coordinated and in the same tone as the hat.

Evening wear was set off by a small clutch purse in satin or leather or a small pouch-shaped purse in brocade or velvet with a chain handle. Bakelite trimmings were also very "of the moment."

GLOVES

In keeping with the general formality of the period, gloves were worn almost everywhere. They came in over-the-wrist length in suede or leather for day wear and in elbow-length satin for evenings. Gauntlet-style gloves with decorative panels were also popular. A popular trim was three lines of stitching running from between the fingers on the back of the hand. This lent a touch of elegance to the plainest pair.

Below: This neat little purse-compact, probably made of Bakelite, has a typical art deco design of diamanté chevrons.

Knitted Fair Isle pattern wool gloves were worn for all kinds of winter sports and in the country. Men's gloves came in black or brown soft leather and were especially worn for driving.

JEWELRY

The costume jewelry of the 1930s was some of the most elegant yet designed. In keeping with the more serious style of clothing, there was a return to more traditional pieces. Materials included everything from gold, silver, and the newly fashionable "white metal"—platinum—to plastic, chrome, and Bakelite. In the early years, pieces followed the geometric lines of art deco, the most typical being diamanté clip earrings in a sunburst shape and a straight, narrow pin with diamanté trim. American designers such as Tiffany established their iconic status with these styles. Red, black, white, and silver were keynote colors. Later in the decade, however, jewelry lost its hard edges and became more curvy and feminine. Flower sprays with semiprecious stones such as rubies and emeralds were popular, as were paste, turquoise, and marcasite.

At the other end of the spectrum, there was a craze for fun Bakelite pieces in the shape of Scottie dogs, cats, fawns, parrots—even a frog playing a banjo. Lobsters, the surrealists' favorite creature, also featured frequently among these brightly colored pieces, which were worn on coats and jackets.

WATCHES

Wristwatches were very fashionable and were worn as much for their decorative effect as their practical purpose. For a woman in evening dress, a narrow bracelet-style watch with a square or oblong face in platinum set with tiny diamonds and rubies looked fabulous and twinkled in the light. For men, wristwatches had now replaced pocket watches for general wear. The most popular men's styles also had square or oblong faces but came in a more manly size and with a mock-croc strap. The faces of all these watches were set with hands and neat numerals: digital watches weren't even on the drawing board and are definitely out!

Below: These fabulous art deco watches, in a variety of typical shapes, are real collectors' items. They would have had narrow bracelets of braided leather, silk cord, or metal links.

HAIR AND MAKEUP

Not everybody went peroxide blonde, but it was a very popular look among women between the ages of 20 and 30 who based their style on the movies. Hair was generally short and set in permanent waves or tight, glossy pin curls, which meant regular visits to the hairdresser. A Garbo-style shoulder-length waved bob was less trouble and was considered very sexy, especially when it fell over one eye and lent an air of mystery. Longer hair was worn in a pleat or chignon for evening glamour. The straight-cut bob, symbol of 1920s rebellion, was now very unfashionable.

Makeup was pale, toning from ivory to blush pink, even sometimes a greenish tone, and was intended to convey a more naturally elegant image than the obviously "made-up" look of the 1920s. Advertisements made much of finding the exact shade to suit a woman's complexion, with products named "Gardenia" (ivory pale) and "Tea Rose" (with a touch of pink). A soft dab of rouge was applied to the "apple" of the cheeks, like today's blush. Eyebrows were plucked to a fine line and sometimes drawn on, and false eyelashes were sometimes used. Eye shadow was bright and shimmering for evenings, smoldering brown or gray for daytime, with perhaps just a slick of Vaseline to give shine.

Lipstick, applied generously to make the mouth appear full and rounded, came in raspberry and orange tones in the early 1930s, shading to brighter red by the end of the decade. Nail polish came in every shade of red and, by the end of the decade, also in more daring shades to match a dress—green, pearl gray, or metallic. However, nail polish took longer to catch on than other cosmetics, so if you're representing a particular look, check the dates carefully. Note, though, that at this time, nail polish was applied only to the center part of the nail, leaving the cuticle and tip unpainted. In general, costumers should not have much trouble with the makeup of this period; just remember not to go over the top. And although 1930s women patiently applied layers of foundation, rouge, and powder, today's cosmetics will give the right look with far less effort.

Below: Applying lipstick in public was no longer considered vulgar in the 1930s. However, whether or not this woman can see through her ultra-fashionable sunglasses is debatable!

argyle pattern Diamond shapes set in a diagonal checkerboard arrangement.

Bakelite The first plastic made from synthetic components. Non-conductive and heat-resistant, it was used in industry and the kitchen as well as in jewelry and toys.

batiste A soft, lightweight, opaque fabric made of woven cotton.

bias cut Fabric cut not on the straight grain but at an angle of 45 degrees. This gives it a natural stretch.

bolero A very short jacket with sleeves, just covering the shoulders. Similar to the modern "shrug."

box pleat A double pleat made by turning under fabric on both sides.

brocade A rich, heavy fabric with a raised design woven into it.

bugle beads Narrow, tubular glass beads.

chiffon A sheer crepe fabric made by twisting the yarn: usually made of silk or nylon.

couture High-fashion garments, usually made to order.

crepe A fabric with a wrinkled surface.

culottes A long divided skirt that gives the same freedom of movement as pants.

cummerbund A broad sash worn around the waist.

diamanté Sparkling stone resembling a diamond.

directoire knickers Knee-length knickers, elasticized at waist and knee.

Fair Isle pattern Traditional knitting style, using multiple colors, which originated on Fair Isle off northern Scotland.

georgette Lightweight fabric, originally made from silk, with a crinkly crepe-like texture.

handkerchief hem A hemline falling in points like a handkerchief.

jersey A cotton or cotton-blend knitted fabric.

lamé A fabric interwoven with metal threads that give a metallic sheen.

marabou Very fine, fluffy feathers.

marcasite A form of iron sulfide often used in inexpensive jewelry to imitate diamonds.

muslin A very finely woven cotton fabric.

nylon A synthetic material developed in 1935 as a cheaper replacement for silk.

organdie (or organdy) A lightweight fabric similar to batiste but more transparent.

poplin A medium-weight fabric with a slightly ribbed texture, made of cotton or cotton blend.

rayon A high-sheen synthetic fabric, made from wood pulp. Also known as "art silk" or "viscose."

rouge Red powder or cream used to give color to the cheeks.

satin A medium-weight silky fabric with a glossy surface and a dull reverse.

sequins Tiny circles of metal or plastic foil used to decorate garments.

serge A twill fabric, usually of wool or worsted, with a diagonal ribbed texture.

shawl collar A collar whose lapels descend in a curved line without notches.

shingle A short haircut, slightly waved and tapered to a V shape at the nape of the neck.

smocking Decorative stitching worked over gathered fabric, usually on the bodice of a dress.

spats A kind of shoe-protector that buttons on over the ankle.

swagger coat A triangular-shaped coat with a flared back and raglan sleeves.

toque A small, round brimless hat worn by women.

trench coat A knee-length belted raincoat, based on military design.

tulle A fine net fabric made of silk or rayon.

tweed A closely woven, unfinished wool fabric with a rough texture, originating in Scotland.

winged collar A small standing collar with the points bent outward to resemble wings.

Further Information

BOOKS

GENERAL

Dearling, Shirley. *Elegantly Frugal Costumes: The Poor Man's Do-It-Yourself Costume Maker's Guide.* Meriwether, 1992.

Haley, Gail E. *Costumes for Plays and Playing.* Parkway, 2002.

Holkeboer, Katherine Strand. *Patterns for Theatrical Costumes: Garments, Trims, and Accessories from Ancient Egypt to 1915.* Drama Publishers, 1993.

Kidd, Mary. *Stage Costume, Step by Step.* Betterway Books, 2002.

La Motte, Richard. *Costume Design 101: The Business and Art of Creating Costumes for Film and Television.* Michael Wiese Productions, 2001.

Leese, Elizabeth. *Costume Design in the Movies: An Illustrated Guide to the Work of 157 Great Designers.* Dover, 1991.

Pecktal, Lynn. *Costume Design: Techniques of Modern Masters.* Backstage Books, 1999.

Rogers, Barb. *Costuming Made Easy: How to Make Theatrical Costumes from Cast-Off Clothing.* Meriwether, 1999.

PERIOD

Altman & Co. *1920s Fashions from B. Altman & Co.* Dover, 1998.

Blum, Stella. *Everyday Fashions of the Thirties as Featured in Sears and Other Catalogues.* Dover, 1981.

Blum, Stella. *Everyday Fashions of the Twenties as Featured in Sears and Other Catalogues.* Dover, 1981.

Grafton, Carol Belanger. *Fashions of the Thirties: 476 Copyright-Free Illustrations.* Dover, 1993.

Peacock, John. *The 1930s: Fashion Sourcebook.* Thames & Hudson, 1997.

Peacock, John. *Fashion Accessories: The Complete 20th Century Sourcebook.* Thames & Hudson, 2000.

Peacock, John. *20th Century Jewellery: The Complete Sourcebook.* Thames & Hudson, 2002.

Schiaparelli, Elsa. *Shocking Life.* V&A Publications, 2007.

Ward, Tammy. *Fashionable Clothing from the Sears Catalogs: Early 1930s.* Schiffer Publishing, 2007.

Ward, Tammy. *Fashionable Clothing from the Sears Catalogs: Mid 1930s.* Schiffer Publishing, 2007.

WEB SITES

www.bombshells.com
Gallery of publicity photos of actresses in costume.

www.costumes.org/history/100pages/ mensfashhist.htm
Good illustrations of men's wear advertising of the period.

www.evadress.com
Has vintage patterns, 1800s to 1950s, in a range of sizes.

www.fashion-era.com/stylish_thirties.htm
General information on styles of clothing.

www.thefedoralounge.com
Information on hats and hairstyles.

www.hairarchives.com
Information on hairstyles and beauty in general.

www.lib.berkeley.edu/MRC/2030svid.html# movies
Has good information on movies of the period.

www.1930s-fashions.co.uk
Excellent period illustrations of the fashions of the time.

Source List

A selection of plays, movies, TV series and musicals with 1920s and 1930s themes.

THE TWENTIES

PLAYS

Chicago (1926), by Maurine Dallas Watkins

Chicago (1975), musical, by Kander and Ebb

The Front Page (1931), by Ben Hecht

Hay Fever (1925), by Noel Coward

Ma Rainey's Black Bottom (1982), by August Wilson

Once in a Lifetime (1929-30), by Moss Hart and George S. Kaufman

MOVIES AND TV

The Blue Angel (1930), dir. Josef von Sternberg, with Emil Jannings, Marlene Dietrich

Bonnie and Clyde (1967), dir. Arthur Penn, with Faye Dunaway, Warren Beatty

The Cat's Meow (2001), dir. Peter Bogdanovich, with Kirsten Dunst, Edward Herrmann

Chariots of Fire (1981), dir. Hugh Hudson, with Ian Charleson, Ben Cross

Chicago (2002), dir. Rob Marshall, with Catherine Zeta-Jones, Renée Zellweger

The Cotton Club (1984), dir. Francis Ford Coppola, with Richard Gere, Gregory Hines

The Flapper (1920), dir. Alan Crosland, with Olive Thomas, Warren Cook

The Godfather Part 2 (1974), dir. Francis Ford Coppola, with Robert De Niro, Al Pacino

The Great Gatsby (1974), dir. Jack Clayton, with Mia Farrow, Robert Redford

The Great Gatsby (2000, TV), dir. Robert Markowitz, with Mia Sorvino, Toby Stephens

The Hours (2002), dir. Stephen Daldry, with Nicole Kidman, Julianne Moore

The Moderns (1988), dir. Alan Rudolph, with Keith Carradine, Linda Fiorentino

Mrs Dalloway (1997), dir. Marleen Gorris, with Vanessa Redgrave, Rupert Graves

Mrs Parker and the Vicious Circle (1994), dir. Alan Rudolph, with Jennifer Jason Leigh, Campbell Scott

Once in a Lifetime (1932), dir. Russell Mack, with Jack Oakie, Sidney Fox

Once Upon a Time in America (1984), dir. Sergio Leone, with Robert De Niro, James Woods

Out of Africa (1985), dir. Sydney Pollack, with Meryl Streep, Robert Redford

The Painted Veil (1934), dir. Ryszard Boleslawski, with Greta Garbo, Herbert Marshall

The Painted Veil (2006), dir. John Curran, with Naomi Watts, Edward Norton

A Passage to India (1985), dir. David Lean, with Peggy Ashcroft, Judy Davis

Singin' in the Rain (1952), dir. Stanley Donan and Gene Kelly, with Gene Kelly, Debbie Reynolds

Thoroughly Modern Millie (1967), dir. George Roy Hill, with Julie Andrews, Mary Tyler Moore

Valentino (1977), dir. Ken Russell, with Rudolf Nureyev, Leslie Caron

Gangster movies

Angels with Dirty Faces (1938), dir. Michael Kurtiz, with James Cagney, Pat O'Brien

Bugsy Malone (1976), dir. Alan Parker, with Jodie Foster, Scott Baio

'G' Men (1935), dir. William Keighley, with James Cagney, Anne Dvorak

Little Caesar (1931), dir. Mervyn LeRoy, with Edward G. Robinson, Douglas Fairbanks Jnr.

Miller's Crossing (1990), dir. Joel Coen, with Gabriel Byrne, Albert Finney

The Public Enemy (1931), dir. William A Wellman, with James Cagney, Jean Harlow

The Roaring Twenties (1939), dir. Raoul Walsh, with James Cagney, Humphrey Bogart

Scarface (1932), dir. Howard Hawks, with Paul Muni, George Raft

The Untouchables (1987), dir. Brian de Palma, with Kevin Costner, Robert De Niro

THE THIRTIES

PLAYS

Awake and Sing (1935), by Clifford Odets

Design for Living (1933), by Noel Coward

Our Town (1938), by Thornton Wilder

Present Laughter (1939), by Noel Coward

Private Lives (1930), by Noel Coward

MOVIES

Annie (1982), dir. John Huston, with Albert Finney, Aileen Quinn

Atonement (2007), dir. Joe Wright, with Keira Knightley, James McAvoy

The Aviator (2004), dir. Martin Scorsese, with Leonardo DiCaprio, Cate Blanchett

Bound for Glory (1976), dir. Hal Ashby, with David Carradine, Ronny Cox

Cabaret (1972), dir. Bob Fosse, with Liza Minnelli, Michael York

Cinderella Man (2005), dir. Ron Howard, with Russell Crowe, Renée Zellweger

Citizen Kane (1941), dir. Orson Welles, with Orson Welles, Joseph Cotten

Death on the Nile (1978), dir. John Guillermin, with Peter Ustinov, Bette Davis

Design for Living (1933), dir. Ernst Lubitsch, with Gary Cooper, Fredric March

A Good Woman (2004), dir. Mike Barker, with Helen Hunt, Scarlett Johansson

Gosford Park (2001), dir. Robert Altman, with Maggie Smith, Eileen Atkins

Grand Hotel (1932), dir. Edmund Goulding, with Greta Garbo, John Barrymore

The Grapes of Wrath (1940), dir. John Ford, with Henry Fonda, John Carradine

His Girl Friday (1940), dir. Howard Hawks, with Cary Grant, Rosalind Russell

I'm No Angel (1933), dir. Wesley Ruggles, with Mae West, Cary Grant

Julia (1977), dir. Fred Zinnemann, with Jane Fonda, Vanessa Redgrave

King Kong (1933), with Fay Wray, Robert Armstrong

King Kong (2005), dir. Peter Jackson, with Naomi Watts, Jack Black

Letty Lynton (1932), dir. Clarence Brown, with Joan Crawford, Robert Montgomery

Murder on the Orient Express (1974), dir. Sidney Lumet, with Albert Finney, Ingrid Bergman

O Brother, Where Art Thou? (2000), dir. Joel Coen, with George Clooney, John Turturro

Paper Moon (1973), dir. Peter Bogdanovich, with Ryan O'Neal, Tatum O'Neal

The Purple Rose of Cairo (1985), dir. Woody Allen, with Mia Farrow, Jeff Daniels

Le Quai des Brumes (1938), dir. Marcel Carné, with Jean Gabin, Michel Simon

La Règle du Jeu (1939), dir. Jean Renoir, with Nora Gregor, Marcel Dalio

Road to Perdition (2002), dir. Sam Mendes, with Tom Hanks, Paul Newman

The Sting (1973), dir. George Roy Hill, with Paul Newman, Robert Redford

Sweet and Lowdown (2000), dir. Woody Allen, with Sean Penn, Samantha Morton

They Shoot Horses, Don't They? (1969), dir. Sydney Pollack, with Jane Fonda, Michael Sarrazin

To Kill a Mockingbird (1962), dir. Robert Mulligan, with Gregory Peck, Mary Badham

Victor/Victoria (1982), dir. Blake Edwards, with Julie Andrews, James Garner

Index

Numbers in **bold** refer to illustrations.